Sleeping Saurus

by Liza Charlesworth
illustrated by Doug Jones

SCHOLASTIC

New York ★ Toronto ★ London ★ Auckland
Sydney ★ Mexico City ★ New Delhi ★ Hong Kong

To a
sweet & zesty kid
named Zach

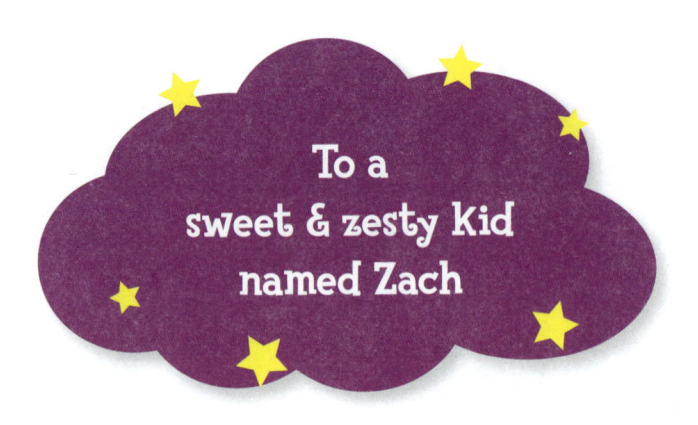

No part of this publication may be reproduced, stored in a retrieval system, or transmitted in any form or by any means, electronic, mechanical, photocopying, recording, or otherwise, without written permission of the publisher. For information regarding permission, write to Scholastic Inc., Attention: Permissions Department, 557 Broadway, New York, NY 10012.

ISBN 978-0-545-68632-7

Copyright © 2011 by Lefty's Editorial Services

All rights reserved. Published by Scholastic Inc.
SCHOLASTIC, LET'S LEARN READERS™, and associated logos are trademarks and/or registered trademarks of Scholastic Inc.

12 11 10 9 8 7 6 5 4 3 2 1   14 15 16 17 18 19/0

Printed in China.

Once upon a time, there lived a king and queen. They ruled Stompville, a leafy land filled with happy dinosaurs.

One day, the queen laid a huge speckled egg. She covered it with leaves to keep it warm. Many months passed, until one day . . .

. . . *crack!* Out popped a very cute baby.

"Our little princess!" said the queen.

"We'll have a big party to celebrate!" said the king.

All the dinosaurs in Stompville came to the party. Everyone fell instantly in love with the princess. Everyone, that is, except the Wicked Witchosaurus. She hated cute babies.

So she cast this evil spell:
"*Hocus Pocus, Tyrannosaurus,*
I put a spell on the princess before us.
At a tender age, she'll be pricked by a claw
And fast asleep, the girl will fall."

Then she added:

"*And the princess shall have such a
  beastly snore,
Nothing will save her forevermore!*"

With that, the Wicked Witchosaurus dashed off and was never seen again.

The king and queen roared in horror.

"What will we do?" asked the queen.

"I know," said the king, "I'll pass a law that every dinosaur in the land must wear mittens. Then, no harm can come to our little princess." And so he did.

The dinosaurs all wore mittens, just as the king had decreed. Years went by. The princess grew up and had lots of fun. She hosted tea-rex parties. She played hide-and-creep. She got her tail done.

She even dinosat. One day, a little raptor dropped his mitten. When the princess handed it back to him—*Ouch!* She got pricked by his claw.

Crash! The princess toppled over and fell fast asleep.

Snore, snore, snore! Just as the Wicked Witchosaurus had promised, the princess had a loud, beastly snore.

The snoring was louder than whirling tornadoes. It was louder than erupting volcanoes. It was so loud that no one in the land could sleep a single wink.

For years, the princess snoozed and snored. For years, the dinosaurs tried to wake her up. They roared. They stomped. They tickled her tummy. Nothing worked.

Then something magical happened. The snoring reached the ear of a handsome prince in a faraway land.

"What's that lovely sound?" he said. "I must find out where it's coming from."

He walked for miles. With each step, the snoring grew louder. *Snore, snore, snore!*

After many days, he reached Stompville. He could not believe his eyes. Everyone was sleepy, grumpy, *and* wearing mittens.

"What a strange land!" he exclaimed. He crept closer to the beautiful snoring.

At last, he found what he'd been searching for! On a bed of flowers, lay a princess with scaly skin, pink spots, and the loudest snore in the world.

"Please wake her up," said the queen.

"Her snoring is driving us crazy," said the king.

So the prince knelt down and kissed the girl's pretty lips. Her giant eyes popped open—it was love at first sight.

"My darling, Sleeping Saurus, will you marry me?" asked the prince.

"Yes!" said the princess with a joyful yawn.

"They're a great match," said the queen.

"It's finally quiet," said the king.

Then they both fell fast asleep. *Crash, crash!* So did all the other dinosaurs in the land. *Crash, crash, crash!*

After their naps, the dinosaurs took off their mittens and cheered. *Hip hip hooray!* The Wicked Witchosaurus's evil spell was finally broken!

The prince and princess had a dinomite wedding! There was music and stomping and yummy cake. And everyone lived happily ever after.

Comprehension Boosters

1. Retell this story in your own words.

2. Why does the king pass a law to make all the dinosaurs in Stompville wear mittens?

3. Why can't any of the dinosaurs in Stompville fall asleep?

4. Can you think of five great words to describe the dinosaur princess? How about the Wicked Witchosaurus?

5. What happens *after* everyone lives happily ever after? Turn on your imagination and tell a story about it!